ANNA DEL CONTE'S

Italian Kitchen

I RISOTTI

RISOTTOS AND OTHER RICE DISHES

ILLUSTRATED BY FLO BAYLEY

SIMON &
SCHUSTER

SIMON & SCHUSTER

SIMON & SCHUSTER
Simon & Schuster Building
Rockefeller Center
1230 Avenue of the Americas
New York, New York 10020

SIMON & SCHUSTER and colophon are registered trademarks
of Simon & Schuster Inc.
Designed by Andrew Barron & Collis Clements Associates
Typesetting by Selwood Systems, Midsomer Norton
Printed in and bound in Italy by New Interlitho

10 9 8 7 6 5 4 3 2 1

Library of Congress Cataloging in Publication Data:
Del Conte, Anna.
    I risotti : risottos and other appetizers / by Anna del Conte.
        p.   cm.—(Anna del Conte's Italian Kitchen)
    Includes bibliographical references and index.
    ISBN 0–671–87030–0 : $14.00
    1. Cookery (Rice).   2. Cookery, Italian.   I. Title.
II. Series: Del Conte, Anna.   Anna del Conte's Italian Kitchen
TX809.R6D44   1993
641.8'12—dc20   93–13330
                                                        CIP

CONTENTS

RISOTTI

Risotto is a relative newcomer to the Italian culinary scene, where most dishes can trace their origins back to the Renaissance, if not to Roman times. It was only during the nineteenth century that risotto became popular in the northern regions of Italy – Piedmont, Lombardy, and Veneto – where the rice was cultivated, and indeed it still is.

A genuine risotto, for all its apparent simplicity, is a challenge to most cooks. Although there are certain rules to observe, the feel of making a good risotto can only be learned with practice. The first essential is to use top quality ingredients. Secondly, one must remember that risotto is prepared according to a well-defined method. It is not just a mixture of rice and other ingredients, and it is certainly not, as some people have believed, a dish that Italians make from an assortment of leftovers. Rice is often the only ingredient, apart from flavorings. When there are other ingredients they are almost always cooked with the rice, so as to allow the flavors to combine and fuse.

The rice must be medium-grain white rice, which absorbs the liquid it cooks in and swells up without breaking or becoming mushy. Only two types of rice are suitable for making risotto: superfino and fino. Arborio, which is widely available, is the most popular variety of superfino rice and is suitable for all risotti. It has large, plump grains which produce a delicious nutty taste when cooked. Carnaroli, a new superfino variety, is produced in relatively small quantities. It keeps its firm consistency, while its starch dissolves deliciously during the cooking. Vialone Nano, a fino rice, has a shorter, stubbier grain containing starch of a kind that does not soften easily in the cooking. It is my favorite rice for vegetable risotti. Vialone Nano cooks more quickly than

Arborio – 15 minutes, as opposed to 20 minutes for Arborio. Both Carnaroli and Vialone Nano can be found in specialist Italian grocers. In most of the recipes I have specified the best variety of rice to use, bearing in mind availability.

The choice of saucepan is crucial to the success of the dish. The pan must be wide, heavy-bottomed, and large enough to contain the rice when it has finished cooking, by which time it will have increased its volume by nearly three times. Ideally it should also be round-bottomed, to prevent the rice from sticking in the corners.

The quality of the broth is also very important. It should be a good, but light, meat broth, made with a piece of veal, some beef, one or two pieces of chicken, and very few bones, all flavored with vegetables, herbs, and seasonings. Pork and lamb are never used for this kind of broth. Vegetable broth is particularly suitable for a vegetable or fish risotto; for the latter a light fish broth is also good. If you have no broth already prepared, use good quality chicken or beef bouillon cubes; there are some on the market that do not contain monosodium glutamate.

Good quality Italian rice takes about 15–20 minutes to cook, according to the variety. At the end of the cooking the rice should be *al dente* – firm but tender without a chalky center – and the risotto should have a creamy consistency.

You will find here recipes for 12 risotti, many with vegetables, others with fish and with meat. These last are more nourishing and are definitely main course dishes, while the lighter risotti with vegetables can be the start, *all'Italiana*, of any dinner party.

Risotto should be eaten as soon as it is done, but if you do not like to cook when your guests have already arrived, you can make a *timballo* instead, and accompany it with a suitable sauce if you wish. For this, keep the risotto slightly undercooked, being careful to add the broth very gradually at the end of the cooking or the rice will be too liquid when it is ready. Spread the risotto out on a large dish and let it cool. When it is cold, spoon it into a ring mold that has been generously buttered and sprinkled with dry bread crumbs. Set the mold in a water bath (a roasting pan containing water) and bake in the oven heated to 425°F for about 20 minutes. Loosen the risotto all around the mold with a long metal spatula. Place a large, round platter over it and turn the whole thing upside-down. Give the mold a few taps on the top, shake the platter and mold vigorously, and lift the mold away. If some of the risotto sticks to the mold, remove it and patch up the shape neatly. Nobody will notice, especially if you place some bits of basil or parsley over it.

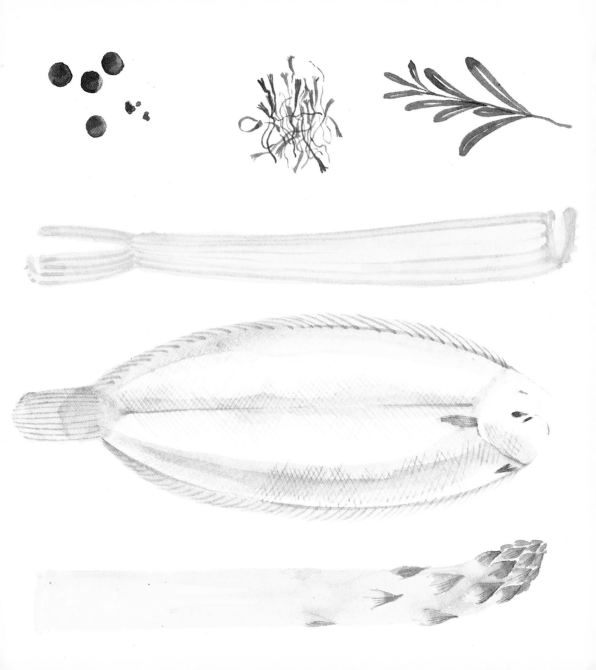

RISOTTO IN BIANCO

RISOTTO WITH PARMESAN

Serves 4–5 as a first course or
as an accompaniment

1½ quarts light meat broth
2 shallots or 1 small onion, very
finely chopped
4 tablespoons unsalted butter
1½ cups Italian rice, preferably
Carnaroli or Arborio
½ cup freshly grated Parmesan
cheese
salt and freshly ground
black pepper

This is the basic risotto and, as such, the purest of any. It is the one that, during the truffle season, is crowned with slivers of white truffle. In Italy, it is mostly eaten by itself, but you can serve it as an accompaniment to meat.

1 Bring the broth to a gentle simmer, keep it simmering all through the cooking of the rice.

2 Meanwhile, put the shallots or onion in a heavy-bottomed saucepan with half the butter. Sauté until translucent and soft, about 7 minutes.

3 Add the rice and stir until well coated with the butter. Sauté, stirring constantly with a wooden spoon, until the grains become partly translucent and the rice begins to stick to the bottom of the pan, 1–2 minutes.

4 Now pour over about $\frac{2}{3}$ cup of the simmering broth. Stir very thoroughly and cook until the rice has absorbed nearly all the broth, then add another ladleful. Continue to add broth gradually, and in small quantities, so that the rice always cooks in liquid but is never drowned by it. Stir constantly at first; after the first two ladlefuls, you need to stir frequently but not all the time. In Milan, we say that a good risotto should just 'catch' at the bottom. The heat should be medium, so as to keep the rice at a steady and lively simmer. If you run out of broth before the rice is cooked, add some boiling water.

5 When the rice is *al dente* (good rice takes at least 15 minutes), remove the pan from the heat. Add the rest of the butter, cut into small pieces, the Parmesan, and seasoning to taste and put the lid firmly on the pan. Let rest 1 minute, until the butter and Parmesan have melted, and then give the risotto a vigorous stir. Serve at once, with more Parmesan passed separately in a bowl.

This dish can easily become a risotto with dried porcini. Pour $\frac{2}{3}$ cup of very hot water over 1 ounce of dried porcini. Let soak 30 minutes and then lift them out and rinse under cold water. Dry well. Chop them finely and add them to the shallots or onion. Sauté them 1 minute before you add the rice, then proceed according to the recipe above. Filter the liquid in which the porcini have soaked through a strainer lined with cheesecloth and add it to the rice while it is cooking.

RISOTTO AL LIMONE

RISOTTO WITH LEMON

Serves 4 as a first course or 3 as a main course

5 cups homemade light meat or vegetable broth
4 tablespoons unsalted butter
1 tablespoon olive oil
2 shallots, very finely chopped
1 celery stalk very finely chopped
$1\frac{1}{4}$ cups Italian rice, preferably Arborio
$\frac{1}{2}$ unwaxed lemon
5 or 6 fresh sage leaves
leaves from a small sprig of fresh rosemary
1 egg yolk
$\frac{1}{4}$ cup freshly grated Parmesan cheese
$\frac{1}{4}$ cup whipping cream
salt and freshly ground black pepper

This recipe was in my book, *Secrets from an Italian Kitchen*. Friends and reviewers alike have all said they found it one of the best risotti ever, which is why I feel no qualms about repeating it here.

1 Bring the broth to a gentle simmer (keep it simmering all through the cooking of the rice).

2 Heat half the butter, the oil, shallots, and celery in a heavy-bottomed saucepan and sauté until the *soffritto* – frying mixture – of shallot and celery is softened, about 7 minutes. Mix in the rice and continue to sauté, stirring, until the rice is well coated with the butter and is partly translucent, 1–2 minutes.

3 Pour over about $\frac{2}{3}$ cup of the simmering broth. Stir very thoroughly and cook until the rice has absorbed nearly all of the broth, still stirring. Add another ladleful of simmering broth, and continue in this manner until the rice is ready. You may not need all the broth. Good quality Italian rice for risotto takes 15–20 minutes to cook.

4 Meanwhile, thinly pare the zest from the lemon half and chop it with the herbs. Mix into the rice halfway through the cooking.

5 Squeeze the half lemon into a small bowl and combine it with the egg yolk, Parmesan, cream, a little salt, and a very generous grinding of black pepper. Mix well with a fork.

6 When the rice is *al dente*, remove the pan from the heat and stir in the egg and cream mixture and the remaining butter. Cover the pan and let rest 2 minutes or so. Then give the risotto an energetic stir, transfer to a heated dish or bowl, and serve at once, with more grated Parmesan in a little bowl if you wish.

RISOTTO ALLA MILANESE

RISOTTO WITH SAFFRON

Serves 4–5 as a first course or as an accompaniment

1½ quarts homemade light meat broth
1 small onion, very finely chopped
5 tablespoons unsalted butter
1½ cups Italian rice, preferably Carnaroli
¾ cup good red wine
½ teaspoon powdered saffron or saffron strands crushed to a powder
salt and freshly ground black pepper
⅔ cup freshly grated Parmesan cheese

Some Italians have queried the use of red wine instead of white in this recipe. My answer is that not only in my own family – Milanese for generations – but in some very authoritative books the wine suggested is red. Other recipes do not include any wine, but add some cream or milk at the end. The choice is yours.

As for the saffron, the strands are definitely more reliable than the powder, but they must be added earlier in the cooking so as to dissolve well, thus losing some flavor during the cooking.

This is the risotto traditionally served with Ossobuco and with Costolette alla Milanese, breaded veal chops.

1 Bring the broth to simmering point (keep it at a very low simmer all through the cooking of the rice).
2 Put the onion and 4 tablespoons of the butter in a heavy-bottomed saucepan and sauté until soft and translucent. Add the rice and stir until well coated with butter. Sauté until the rice is partly translucent, 1–2 minutes. Pour in the wine and boil 1 minute, stirring constantly, then pour in ⅔ cup of the simmering broth. Cook until nearly all the broth has been absorbed and then add another ladleful of the simmering broth. Continue cooking and adding small quantities of broth, while keeping the risotto at a steady lively simmer all the time. If you finish the broth before the rice is properly cooked, add a little boiling water.
3 About halfway through the cooking (good rice takes about 15–20 minutes to cook), add the saffron dissolved in a little broth. When the rice is *al dente*, taste and adjust the seasoning.
4 Remove the pan from the heat and mix in the rest of the butter and 4 tablespoons of the Parmesan. Put the lid on and let rest 1

minute or so. When the butter and the Parmesan have melted, give the risotto a vigorous stir and transfer to a heated dish. Serve immediately, with the rest of the cheese passed separately.

RISOTTO AL POMODORO

RISOTTO WITH TOMATOES

The match of risotto with tomatoes is a modern one, but it is so good that I am sure it will become a classic. This risotto does not contain any butter. It is very light and fresh, and it is very good, if not better, cold.

Serves 4 as a first course or 3 as a main course

1½ pounds ripe tomatoes, peeled
7 tablespoons extra virgin olive oil
3 or 4 garlic cloves, thickly sliced
a good handful of fresh basil leaves, torn into pieces
5 cups vegetable broth
1¼ cups Italian rice, preferably Carnaroli
salt and freshly ground black pepper

1 Cut the peeled tomatoes in half. Squeeze out and discard some of the seeds. Chop the tomatoes coarsely and put them in a heavy-bottomed saucepan large enough to hold the rice later. Remember that the rice will be nearly three times its original volume by the end of the cooking.

2 Add 4 tablespoons of the oil to the pan, then add the garlic and half the basil. Cook briskly 1–2 minutes, stirring.

3 Meanwhile, bring the broth to a simmer (keep it simmering very gently all through the making of the risotto).

4 Add the rice to the pan with the tomatoes and cook about 2 minutes, stirring constantly.

5 Pour over a ladleful of simmering broth and continue cooking, adding more broth little by little until the rice is *al dente*. If you want to serve the risotto cold, remove it from the heat when the rice is slightly underdone; it finishes cooking as it cools.

6 Add salt and pepper to taste and mix in the rest of the oil. Transfer to a serving dish and sprinkle the remaining basil leaves on the top. If you serve the risotto cold, fluff it up with a fork before bringing it to the table.

RISOTTO AL FINOCCHIO

RISOTTO WITH FENNEL

Serves 4–5 as a first course or
3–4 as a main course

2 fennel bulbs, about 1¼ pounds
1 tablespoon olive oil
4 tablespoons unsalted butter
1 small onion, finely chopped
1 celery stalk, finely chopped
5 cups vegetable broth
salt and freshly ground
black pepper
1¼ cups Italian rice, preferably
Vialone Nano
6 tablespoons dry white
¼ cup whipping cream
½ cup freshly grated Parmesan
cheese

Vegetable risotti are one of the great strengths of Venetian cooking. Of all of them, this fennel risotto is my favorite, especially when I can get hold of fennel that is full of flavor and not 'the commercial variety grown in Italy for export which is beautiful but dumb,' as the late Jane Grigson so aptly put it in her splendid *Vegetable Book*.

1 Cut off and discard the fennel stems, but keep some of the feathery green foliage. Remove any bruised outer leaves and then cut the bulbs lengthwise in half. Slice the halves across very finely. Wash thoroughly and drain.

2 Put the oil, half the butter, the onion, and celery in a small sauté pan. Sauté until the vegetables are pale gold. Add the sliced fennel and stir it over and over to let it take up the flavor. Add about 4 tablespoons of the broth and cover the pan. Cook, stirring occasionally, until the fennel is very soft, about 20 minutes. Mash it with a fork to a purée over high heat, so that the excess liquid evaporates. Add salt to taste.

3 Bring the remaining broth to a gentle simmer (keep it simmering all through the cooking of the rice).

4 Heat the remaining butter in a heavy-bottomed saucepan. When the butter foam begins to subside, mix in the rice and stir to coat the grains thoroughly. Sauté until the rice is partly translucent, 1–2 minutes. Turn the heat up and add the wine. Let it bubble away, stirring the rice constantly.

5 Now begin to add the simmering broth, a ladleful at a time. When nearly all of the first ladleful has been absorbed, add another, always stirring the rice. If you run out of broth before the rice is done, add some boiling water and continue the cooking.

6 Halfway through the cooking of the rice, stir in the mashed fennel with all the cooking juices.

7 When the rice is *al dente*, remove the pan from the heat and add the cream, Parmesan, and a generous grinding of pepper. Mix everything together. Transfer to a heated dish, scatter the reserved fennel foliage, previously snipped, over the top, and serve at once.

RISOTTO AL PEPERONE

RISOTTO WITH SWEET PEPPERS

Serves 4 as a first course or 3
as a main course

6 tablespoons extra virgin
olive oil
2 garlic cloves, sliced
3 tablespoons chopped fresh
parsley
4 tomatoes, peeled, seeded,
and chopped
2 large sweet peppers,
preferably 1 yellow and 1 red
5 cups vegetable broth
$1\frac{1}{4}$ cups Italian rice, preferably
Arborio or Vialone Nano
4 pinches of chili powder
salt and freshly ground
black pepper
12 fresh basil leaves

Risotto, the staple of northern Italy, used never to be made with olive oil, the cooking fat of the south. But a few modern risotti are now made very successfully with oil, and with ingredients, in this case sweet peppers, whose ideal dressing is oil.

This is my adaptation of a traditional risotto from Voghera, a town in southwest Lombardy that is famous for its peppers.

1 Heat 4 tablespoons of the oil in a heavy-bottomed saucepan with the garlic and parsley. When the garlic and parsley begin to sizzle, add the chopped tomatoes and cook 5 minutes, stirring frequently.

2 Meanwhile wash and dry the sweet peppers. Peel them, using swivel-headed vegetable peeler. You should "saw" from side to side with it as you peel, rather than sliding it straight down the pepper. If you find them difficult to peel, leave the skin on. Discard the cores, seeds, and white ribs, and cut the peppers into small cubes.

3 Add the peppers to the pan and cook 10 minutes, stirring frequently.

4 Meanwhile, bring the broth to a simmer in another pan. (keep it just simmering all through the cooking). Add the rice to the tomato and pepper mixture and stir very well, letting it absorb the juices. After 1–2 minutes, begin to add the simmering broth by the ladleful. Wait to add each subsequent ladleful until the previous one has nearly all been absorbed.

5 When the rice is *al dente*, about 18 minutes, add the chili powder and salt and pepper to taste. Remove the pan from the heat and stir in the remaining 2 tablespoons of oil. Transfer to a heated deep serving dish, sprinkle with the basil leaves, and serve at once.

RISOTTO ALLA PAESANA
RISOTTO WITH VEGETABLES

This lovely fresh risotto is best made in the spring, when the new peas and asparagus are in season. The vegetable ingredients can vary: you can put in a little celery and carrot when there is no asparagus; green beans are suitable, too. Try to match the flavors of the vegetables so as not to have a strident note.

Serves 4 as a first course or 3 as a main course

$\frac{2}{3}$ cup shelled fresh peas
$\frac{1}{2}$ pound asparagus
$\frac{1}{4}$ pound zucchini
$\frac{1}{2}$ pound ripe, firm tomatoes, peeled, or 1 cup canned Italian plum tomatoes, drained
$\frac{1}{4}$ cup extra virgin olive oil
a bunch of fresh parsley, chopped
1 garlic clove, chopped
salt and freshly ground black pepper
5 cups chicken or vegetable broth
2 tablespoons unsalted butter
2 shallots, chopped
$1\frac{1}{2}$ cup Italian rice, preferably Vialone Nano
$\frac{1}{3}$ cup dry white wine
6 tablespoons freshly grated Parmesan cheese
12 fresh basil leaves, torn into pieces

1 Cook the fresh peas in lightly salted boiling water until just tender. Meanwhile, trim and wash the asparagus and cook them in boiling salted water until *al dente*. Drain and cut the tender part of the spears into small pieces. (Reserve the rest, for a soup or a mousse.) Blanch the zucchini 2–3 minutes, then drain and cut into small cubes. Cut the tomatoes in half, squeeze out the seeds, and then cut into short strips.

2 Put half the oil, the parsley, and garlic in a sauté pan and sauté 1 minute. Stir in all the vegetables, season lightly with salt, and sauté 2 minutes over low heat for them to take the flavor of the *soffritto* – the fried mixture. Set aside.

3 Heat the broth in a saucepan until just simmering (keep it simmering all through the cooking of the rice).

4 Put the rest of the oil and half the butter in a heavy-bottomed saucepan. Add the shallots and sauté until tender. Add the rice and stir until coated, then cook until partly translucent, 1–2 minutes. Splash with the wine and boil rapidly to evaporate, stirring constantly. Add a ladleful of simmering broth and let the rice absorb it while you stir constantly. Continue to add the broth gradually, stirring frequently, until the rice is *al dente*. (This will take about 15 to 20 minutes, according to the quality of the rice.)

5 Halfway through the cooking, stir in the vegetables with all

their cooking juices. Season with pepper; taste to check the salt.
6 When the rice is done, remove the pan from the heat and add the rest of the butter, cut into small pieces and the Parmesan. Place the lid tightly on the pan and let rest 1–2 minutes. Then stir vigorously and transfer to a heated dish. Garnish with the basil leaves and serve at once.

RISOTTO COI PEOCI

RISOTTO WITH MUSSELS

Serves 4 as a first course or 3 as a main course

4 pounds mussels
$1\frac{1}{4}$ cups dry white wine
$\frac{1}{4}$ cup chopped fresh parsley, preferably flat-leaf Italian
6 tablespoons olive oil
3 shallots or 1 medium onion, very finely chopped
salt and freshly ground black pepper
1 quart light fish or vegetable broth
1 celery stalk, with the leaves if possible
1 garlic clove
$\frac{1}{2}$ small dried chili pepper, crumbled
$1\frac{1}{4}$ cups Italian rice, preferably Arborio or Vialone Nano

I have always found a risotto with mussels to be rather unsatisfactory, because you either have only risotto in your mouth, albeit fish-tasting, or else a large mussel. So one day I came up with the idea of chopping up most of the mussels so that morsels of them could be enjoyed in each mouthful. This is the recipe I developed and it works very well.

1 First clean the mussels. Scrape off the barnacles, tug off the beard, and scrub thoroughly with a stiff brush under running water. Throw away any mussel that remains open after you have tapped it on a hard surface; this means it's dead.
2 Put the wine in a large sauté pan, add the mussels, and cover the pan. Cook over high heat until the mussels are open, which will only take 3–4 minutes. Shake the pan every now and then.
3 As soon as the mussels are open, remove the meat from the shells and discard the shells. Strain the cooking liquid through a strainer lined with cheesecloth, pouring it slowly and gently so that the sand will be left at the bottom of the pan.
4 Set aside a dozen of the nicest mussels; chop the rest and put in a bowl. Mix in the parsley.

5 Pour the oil into a heavy-bottomed saucepan. Add the shallots or onion and a pinch of salt and sauté until the shallot is soft and just beginning to color.

6 In another saucepan, heat the broth to simmering point (keep it just simmering all through the cooking of the rice).

7 Meanwhile, chop the celery and garlic together. Add to the shallot with the chili pepper. Sauté 1 minute or so longer. Now add the rice and stir to coat with oil, then cook until partly translucent, 1–2 minutes. Pour over the mussel liquid and stir well. When the liquid has been absorbed add the simmering broth, one ladleful at a time. Stir constantly at first. When the rice is nearly cooked, mix in the chopped mussels, then continue cooking until *al dente*.

8 Season with salt, if necessary, and pepper. Transfer to a heated dish and garnish with the reserved whole mussels.

RISOTTO CON LE ANIMELLE
RISOTTO WITH SWEETBREADS

In restaurants, sweetbreads are often accompanied by boiled rice. That rather boring presentation has, however, led me to devise this dish, where the winey-syrupy sweetbreads are combined with a classic *risotto in bianco*.

During the truffle season, a small white truffle shaved over the top of the risotto makes the dish truly sensational.

1 Soak the sweetbreads in cold water at least 1 hour. Rinse them and put them in a pan with the half lemon and 1 teaspoon of salt. Cover with fresh cold water and bring to a boil. Boil 2 minutes. Drain well, plunge into cold water, and drain again.

Remove all fat and the white tubes, as well as the hard bits. Put the sweetbreads between two plates with a weight on top to squeeze out all excess liquid. Dry them and cut them into morsels.

2 Heat the broth to simmering (keep it simmering all through the cooking of the risotto).

3 Melt half the butter in a heavy-bottomed saucepan. Add the shallots, 4 of the sage leaves, and a pinch of salt and cook until the shallots are soft and translucent.

4 Add the rice and stir to coat with butter then sauté until partly translucent, 1–2 minutes. Pour in the wine and boil 1–2 minutes until it has evaporated, stirring constantly. Now begin to add simmering broth, little by little, in the usual way. Do not add too much at one time or the risotto will not cook properly. Keep the heat lively and constant.

5 Meanwhile, melt half the remaining butter in a sauté or frying pan. Add the rest of the sage leaves. When the sage begins to sizzle, slide in the sweetbreads and sauté 2 minutes, turning them over to brown on all sides. Add the Marsala to the pan and let it bubble away on a low heat. Cook 7–8 minutes, stirring occasionally.

6 When the rice is nearly done, pour the sweetbreads and all the juices into the risotto pan. Stir thoroughly. Taste and adjust the seasoning, and finish cooking the risotto.

7 When the rice is *al dente*, remove the pan from the heat. Add the remaining butter and a couple of spoonfuls of the Parmesan. Cover the pan tightly and let the butter melt 1 minute or so, then stir the risotto gently but thoroughly. Transfer to a heated dish and serve at once, passing the rest of the Parmesan in a bowl.

Serves 4 as a main course

1 pound lamb sweetbreads
$\frac{1}{2}$ lemon
salt and freshly ground black pepper
5 cups light meat broth
1 stick unsalted butter
2 shallots, finely chopped
about 8 fresh sage leaves, snipped
$1\frac{1}{4}$ cups Italian rice, preferably Arborio
6 tablespoons dry white wine
$\frac{1}{4}$ cup Marsala (Madeira or port wine can also be used)
$\frac{2}{3}$ cup freshly grated Parmesan cheese

RISOTTO CON LE SOGLIOLE

RISOTTO WITH DOVER SOLE

Serves 4 as a main course

5 tablespoons unsalted butter
2 tablespoons very finely
chopped shallot
salt and freshly ground
black pepper
5 cups light fish broth
$1\frac{1}{2}$ cups Italian rice,
preferably Carnaroli
$\frac{1}{2}$ cup dry white wine
2 tablespoons chopped fresh dill
$\frac{3}{4}$ pound skinless Dover sole
fillets
$\frac{1}{4}$ cup freshly grated Parmesan
cheese

It might seem extravagant to use Dover sole in a humble dish such as a risotto, but I assure you that it is necessary. You only need a small amount of Dover sole, and it does make a great difference to the dish. The delicacy and firm texture of the fish is in perfect harmony with the soft creaminess of the risotto; none of the other ingredients disturbs this happy balance of flavors.

1 Heat 4 tablespoons of the butter and the shallot in a heavy-bottomed saucepan. Add a pinch of salt and sauté until the shallot is soft and translucent.

2 Meanwhile, heat the fish broth in another saucepan to simmering (keep it at the lowest simmer all through the cooking of the risotto).

3 Add the rice to the shallot and stir to coat with butter, then sauté until partly translucent, 1–2 minutes. Splash with the wine and let it bubble away, stirring constantly.

4 Add about $\frac{2}{3}$ cup of simmering broth, stir well, and let the rice absorb nearly all the liquid. Continue adding broth little by little until the rice is nearly done, then mix in half of the dill and continue the cooking.

5 Meanwhile, heat the remaining butter in a nonstick frying pan. Cut the fish fillets across in half. Slide them into the butter and sauté 3 minutes. Turn them over and sauté 1 minute longer. Sprinkle with salt and pepper.

6 When the rice is *al dente*, mix in the Parmesan and the juices from the fish fillets. Turn into a heated dish. Place the fish fillets neatly over the top and sprinkle with the remaining dill. Serve immediately.

RISOTTO ALLA SCOZZESE
RISOTTO WITH SMOKED SALMON AND
SCOTCH

Serves 4 as a first course or 3
as a main course

4 tablespoons unsalted butter
$\frac{1}{4}$ cup finely chopped shallot
salt
5 cups vegetable or light chicken
broth
$1\frac{1}{4}$ cups Italian rice,
preferably Carnaroli
$\frac{1}{4}$ cup Scotch whisky
$\frac{1}{2}$ pound smoked salmon, cut
into $\frac{3}{4}$-inch pieces
$\frac{1}{3}$ cup whipping cream
2 tablespoons chopped fresh dill
cayenne pepper
freshly grated Parmesan
cheese, for serving

I love smoked salmon and, like most Italians, am not averse to an occasional glass of Scotch. So here I have combined these two very Scottish ingredients with a favorite dish from my home country. This match with a Lombard risotto is particularly successful. The Parmesan is not necessary, but I think its flavor goes well with that of the smoked salmon.

1 Put the butter in a large, heavy-bottomed saucepan. Add the chopped shallot and a pinch of salt; this will release the moisture from the shallot thus preventing it from browning. Sauté until soft and translucent, about 7 minutes.

2 Meanwhile, in another saucepan heat the broth to simmering point (keep it simmering all through the cooking of the rice).

3 Add the rice to the shallot and stir to coat with butter, then cook, until partly translucent, 1–2 minutes. Add the Scotch and let it bubble away, stirring constantly. Add a ladleful of simmering broth and cook the rice on a lively heat, adding a ladleful of broth whenever the rice begins to get dry.

4 When the rice is *al dente*, add the smoked salmon, cream, dill, and cayenne pepper to taste. Mix thoroughly and check the salt before you transfer this delicious risotto to a heated dish. Serve at once, passing the cheese separately in a bowl for those who want it.

RISOTTO CON LA SALSICCIA

RISOTTO WITH SAUSAGE

Some recipes for this dish, originally from Monza (now a suburb of Milan) suggest cutting the sausage in chunks and cooking it separately. In this case the sausage is also served separately and is added to the risotto by each diner. I find this version more suitable if I am serving the risotto as a main course. Here, however, the recipe is for a real risotto, the sausage being added to the rice about 10 minutes before the rice is ready, so that the flavors of the two ingredients will blend thoroughly.

1 Skin the sausage and crumble it. Heat 1 tablespoon of oil and the sage in a nonstick frying pan. Add the sausage and fry briskly 5 minutes, stirring constantly. Pour over the wine, bring to a boil, and cook only enough for the sausage meat to lose its raw color, about 5 minutes.

2 While the sausage is cooking, bring the broth to a simmer (keep it just simmering all through the cooking of the rice).

3 Heat the butter and remaining oil in a heavy-bottomed saucepan. Add the shallots and fry gently until soft and translucent, about 7 minutes.

4 Add the rice to the shallot *soffritto* and cook, stirring constantly, until the grains are partly translucent, 1–2 minutes.

5 Add the simmering broth a ladleful at a time. Wait to add another ladleful until the previous one has nearly all been absorbed.

6 Ten minutes after you start adding the broth, add the sausage and its juice to the rice. Stir well and continue cooking until the rice is *al dente*. Check the seasoning and serve at once, with the Parmesan passed separately if you wish.

Serves 4 as a first course or 3 as a main course

¾ pound luganega sausage or other pure pork, coarse-grained, continental sausage
2 tablespoons olive oil
1 sprig of fresh sage
⅔ cup full-bodied red wine, such as Barbera
5 cups light meat broth
3 tablespoons unsalted butter
2 or 3 shallots, depending on size, finely chopped
1¼ cups Italian rice, preferably Arborio or Carnaroli
salt and freshly ground black pepper
freshly grated Parmesan cheese, for serving (optional)

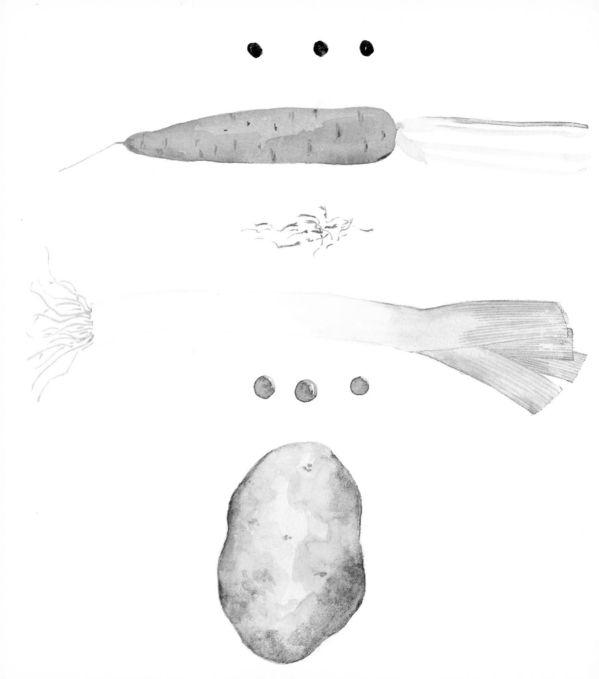

TIMBALLI E PASTICCI DI RISO

MOLDED AND BAKED RICE DISHES

I have included three recipes for this type of rice preparation. There are two elegant molded dishes and a rice, potato, and mussel pie of peasant origin but of great gastronomic merit. All three are particularly suited to dinner parties, since they can be made in advance and then baked in the oven. They are dishes that need a more experienced cook, able to judge the exact cooking time of the different ingredients, and, in the case of the molded dishes, able to shape and unmold the rice. A good point, however, is that cooked rice is very malleable. Should you find yourself with a timballo *tombé* (fallen), you can reshape the rice with your hands and nobody will know. The pie is easy as regards presentation, but requires knowledge in the timing.

SFORMATO DI RISOTTO E PORRI CON LA SALSA DI COZZE

MOLDED LEEK RISOTTO WITH MUSSEL

SAUCE ----

Serves 6 as a first course or 4
as a main course

$2\frac{1}{4}$ pounds mussels
1 tablespoon olive oil
2 garlic cloves
1 thick slice of lemon
$\frac{3}{4}$ pound leeks
5 cups vegetable broth
1 stick unsalted butter
2 cups Italian rice, preferably
Vialone Nano
$1\frac{1}{4}$ cups dry white wine
salt and freshly ground
black pepper
dry bread crumbs for the mold
1 shallot, finely chopped
$\frac{1}{4}$ teaspoon saffron strands (or
saffron powder)
2 teaspoons cornstarch

Leeks and mussels are complementary flavors. The rice here unites them and gives substance to this lovely dish.

1 Scrub the mussels in cold water, knock off the barnacles, and tug off the beard. Rinse in several changes of cold water. Discard any mussel that remains open after you have tapped it against a hard surface.

2 Put the oil, garlic, and slice of lemon in a large sauté pan. Add the mussels, cover the pan, and cook over high heat until the mussels are open, about 4 minutes. Shake the pan very often.

3 Remove the mussel meat from the shells and discard the shells. Filter the liquid through a strainer lined with cheesecloth. Set aside.

4 Cut off the green part of the leeks. Choose the best green leaves, wash them, and blanch in boiling water 2–3 minutes. Drain and cut into $\frac{1}{2}$-inch-wide strips. Set aside.

5 Cut the white part of the leeks into very thin pieces. Wash thoroughly, drain, and dry them.

6 Heat the broth in a saucepan until simmering (keep it simmering all through the making of the risotto).

7 Heat the oven to 350°F.

8 Heat 4 tablespoons of the butter and the white part of the leeks in a large heavy-bottomed saucepan. Sauté until the leeks are just soft and then mix in the rice. Sauté the rice until it is well coated with butter and the grains are partly translucent, 1–2 minutes. Pour over half the wine. Boil briskly 1 minute, stirring constantly.

9 Add a ladleful of the simmering broth and stir well. As soon as nearly all the broth has been absorbed, add another ladleful of broth. Continue cooking the rice in this manner until it is very *al dente*, about 15 minutes. Mix in 2 tablespoons of the butter. Taste and check the seasoning.

10 Very generously butter a 1½-quart cake pan, mold or soufflé dish and coat it with bread crumbs. Spoon the risotto into it, press down gently, and place in the oven while you prepare the sauce.

11 Put the shallot and remaining butter in a saucepan and sauté 5 minutes.

12 Meanwhile, pound the saffron in a mortar. Add 2–3 tablespoons of the mussel liquid and stir thoroughly. Add the cornstarch and stir hard until amalgamated. Pour the mixture into the shallot pan and add the remaining wine and mussel liquid. Bring to a boil very slowly, stirring constantly. Simmer a few minutes for the sauce to thicken and then add the mussels. Add salt and pepper to taste. Cover the pan and remove from the heat.

13 Loosen the risotto from the mold with a long metal spatula. Turn the mold over onto a heated round platter. Tap and shake the mold and then lift it off. Drape the strips of the green part of the leeks over the risotto at regular intervals. Spoon a little of the mussel sauce over the top and pour the rest into a heated bowl. Serve immediately.

ANELLO DI RISOTTO COI E I FUNGHI
RISOTTO RING WITH CHICKEN LIVERS
AND DRIED PORCINI

Serves 6 as a first course or
4–5 as a main course

For the sauce
1 ounce dried porcini
2 tablespoons unsalted butter
5 ounces fresh chicken livers
2 ounces fresh Italian sausage
such as luganega, or Toulouse
sausage, skinned
7 ounces skinned and boned
chicken breast, cut into bite-size
pieces
$\frac{2}{3}$ cup shelled fresh young peas,
or frozen petite peas
2 pinches of ground cloves
$\frac{1}{2}$ cup red wine
salt and freshly ground
black pepper

The plain risotto is served in a ring, the center of which is filled with a rich sauce. It is a showy dish for a dinner party.

1 Soak the dried porcini in very hot water for 30 minutes. Lift them out, rinse them, and dry them. Chop them coarsely. Filter the porcini liquid through a strainer lined with cheesecloth.
2 Heat the butter in a small saucepan. Add the porcini and cook over low heat about 10 minutes.

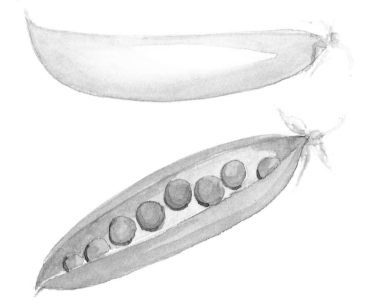

3 Meanwhile, clean the chicken livers, removing all the fat and gristle. Cut into bite-size pieces and put in a small saucepan with the sausage, chicken, and peas. Add the cloves, wine, and salt and pepper to taste. Bring to a boil and cook, uncovered, about 10 minutes, stirring very frequently. Mix in the porcini with all their juices and continue cooking 10 minutes longer. Taste to check the seasoning. Set aside, and reheat before serving.

4 To make the risotto, first bring the broth to a simmer (keep it just simmering all through the cooking of the rice).

5 Heat half the butter with the onion, celery, and carrot in a wide heavy-bottomed saucepan. Cook gently until the vegetables are soft, about 10 minutes, stirring very frequently.

6 Heat the oven to 325°F.

7 Mix the rice into the vegetables and sauté until the grains are partly translucent, 1–2 minutes. Stir in the tomato paste, cook $\frac{1}{2}$ minute, and then pour in the wine. Boil rapidly 1 minute, stirring constantly.

8 Add a ladleful of the simmering broth and 2–3 tablespoons of the porcini liquid. Cook the risotto, gradually adding the remaining broth in the usual way. When the risotto is nearly done and still on the liquid side, remove from the heat. Taste and add salt and pepper. Mix in the rest of the butter and the Parmesan. Cover the pan and leave until the butter has melted, then mix thoroughly.

9 Meanwhile, generously butter a 1-quart ring mold. Coat with bread crumbs, shaking out excess crumbs.

10 Spoon the risotto into the mold. Place the mold in the oven and heat about 10 minutes.

11 Unmold the risotto onto a heated round platter and spoon the hot sauce into the hole.

For the risotto

4 tablespoons unsalted butter
2 tablespoons finely chopped onion
1 tablespoon finely chopped celery
1 tablespoon finely chopped carrot
$1\frac{3}{4}$ cups Italian rice, preferably Vialone Nano
1 tablespoon tomato paste
$\frac{1}{2}$ cup red wine
$1\frac{1}{2}$ quarts chicken broth
salt and freshly ground black pepper
6 tablespoons freshly grated Parmesan cheese
butter and dry bread crumbs for the mold

PATATE, RISO E COZZE DI PIETRO

— POTATO, RICE, AND MUSSEL PIE —

Serves 4 as a main course

4½ pounds mussels
¾ cup dry white wine
1½ pounds boiling potatoes
⅓ cup chopped fresh flat-leaf
Italian parsley
3 teaspoons dried oregano
7 tablespoons extra virgin
olive oil
1 garlic clove, sliced
salt and freshly ground
black pepper
¾ cup Italian rice, preferably
Vialone Nano
1 large zucchini, sliced
½ pound Italian or Bermuda
onion, very finely sliced
⅓ cup grated aged romano
cheese
16 ounces canned Italian
crushed tomatoes

My friend Pietro Pesce is a serious connoisseur of good food. Being a Venetian, he is also a great champion of northern Italian cooking, so that when he came back from Bari, in the south, and gave me this recipe I was quite sure it was worth testing.

The original recipe advises one not to add the mussel juices to the pie because it would make the dish too salty. But when I tested it with Atlantic mussels, less salty and less flavorful than Italian mussels, I decided to add the juices to give the pie the necessary taste of fish and the sea.

1 Scrub the mussels in cold water, knock off the barnacles, and tug off the beard. Rinse in several changes of cold water until there is no sand at the bottom of the sink. Throw away any mussel that is open and remains open after you tap it on a hard surface. It is dead. Set aside a dozen of the best-looking mussels.

2 Put the wine and the remaining mussels in a large sauté pan. Cook, covered, until the mussels open, about 4 minutes. Shake the pan frequently. Remove the mussels as they open or they will toughen. Eventually all the shells containing a mussel will indeed open.

3 Take the meat out of the shells and discard the shells. Filter the mussel liquid through a strainer lined with cheesecloth. You will have about 2½ cups of liquid. Set the meat and the liquid aside in separate bowls.

4 Scrub and wash again the shells of the unshelled mussels and set aside.

5 Peel the potatoes and cut them into wafer-thin slices. I use a food processor fitted with the fine-blade disk. Put the potatoes in

a bowl and toss them with 1 tablespoon of parsley, 1 teaspoon of oregano, 2 tablespoons of oil, a sliver or two of garlic, and a good grinding of pepper.

6 Put the rice in another bowl and the zucchini in a third bowl. Dress each of them with 1 tablespoon of oil, 1 tablespoon of parsley, 1 teaspoon oregano, a sliver or two of garlic, and a grinding of pepper.

7 Heat the oven to 350°F.

8 Choose a shallow metal baking dish no more than 2 inches deep. Grease it well with some of the remaining oil.

9 Spread the onion over the bottom of the dish and cover with the zucchini. Make a layer of half the potatoes and lay all the mussels, shelled and unshelled, over them. Pour about half the mussel liquid into the dish and sprinkle with two-thirds of the cheese. Level down with your hands, and then add the rice and cover with the rest of the potatoes. Pour over the rest of the mussel liquid and season with lots of pepper.

10 Spread the tomatoes, with their juice, all over the top and add enough boiling water to come nearly level with the top of the pie. Sprinkle with the remaining cheese and parsley and 1 teaspoon of salt. (Only a little salt is added because the mussel juices and the romano cheese should have already salted the dish enough.) Drizzle the rest of the oil all over the pie.

11 Cover the pie with foil and bake 1 hour. Remove the foil and continue baking until the potatoes are tender, which depends on their quality and on how thin the slices are. Remove from the oven and let the pie rest 10 minutes before serving, to allow the flavors to blend.

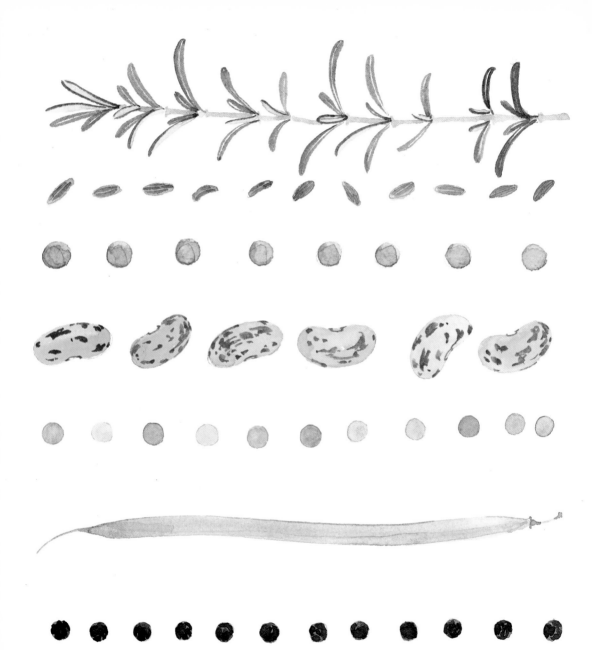

RISI ASCIUTTI E MINESTRE DI RISO

──────── RICE AND VEGETABLE DISHES AND RICE SOUPS ────────

The first two recipes in this section are for dishes that are midway between a soup and a risotto. The rice is boiled in the broth in which the vegetables are cooking, thus the dishes are definitely not risotti. This method of cooking ensures that the taste of the vegetable predominates over the flavor of the rice.

The last three recipes are for soups, all from my home town, Milan, the motherland of good soups. There, most families start their supper with a soup. Often it is a rice soup, which can vary from a rich, earthy minestrone to a sophisticated soup with pieces of chicken, grains of rice and almonds floating in a pale blond pool – a very Chinese-looking soup.

RISI E BISI

RICE WITH PEAS

Serves 4–6 as a first course

1 small onion, very finely chopped
3 tablespoons unsalted butter
1 tablespoon olive oil
1½ pounds young fresh peas, shelled
1½ quarts light meat broth
1 cup Italian rice, preferably Vialone Nano
1 teaspoon fennel seeds, crushed, or 2 tablespoons chopped fresh flat-leaf Italian parsley
⅔ cup freshly grated Parmesan cheese
salt and freshly ground black pepper

The Venetians' love of rice and peas is sublimated in this, the most aristocratic of rice dishes. It was served at the Doge's banquets on the feast of San Marco, April 25th, when the first young peas, grown on the islands of the Venetian lagoon, appear in the market.

This is the old recipe, in which fennel seeds are used instead of parsley.

1 Put the onion, half the butter, and the oil in a heavy-bottomed saucepan and sauté until the onion is pale golden and soft. Mix in the peas and cook over low heat for 10 minutes, adding a few spoonsful of broth during the cooking.

2 Meanwhile, bring the remaining broth to a boil in another saucepan.

3 Add the rice to the peas and sauté, turning the rice over and over, until the grains are partly translucent, 1–2 minutes. Now pour over the boiling broth. Stir well and bring back to a boil. Simmer gently, stirring occasionally, until the rice *al dente*. You might have to add a little more broth during the cooking.

4 A few minutes before the rice is done, add the fennel seeds or parsley, the rest of the butter, and 4 tablespoons of Parmesan. Taste and add salt and pepper to your liking. Stir thoroughly and finish the cooking, then serve at once with the rest of the cheese passed separately.

RISO E LENTICCHIE
—— RICE WITH LENTILS ——

This is an earthy, nourishing soup which I first had one lunchtime in Rome in a busy, bustling trattoria opposite the Quirinale. It was the most lively place imaginable, crowded with civil servants enjoying good homely Roman food.

1 Heat the oil, onion, and pancetta in a heavy-bottomed saucepan. (I use an earthenware pot when I cook legumes.) Sauté, stirring frequently, until the onion is soft but not colored, about 7 minutes.
2 Chop finely the carrot, celery, rosemary leaves, and garlic and mix them together. Add to the onion *soffritto* – frying mixture – and cook over low heat about 10 minutes. Stir frequently. Season with salt and stir in the tomato paste. Cook 1 minute longer.
3 Meanwhile, heat the broth in a separate saucepan.
4 Add the lentils to the vegetable mixture. Stir well and let them *insaporire* – take up the flavor – for 1–2 minutes.
5 Pour enough broth into the pan to cover the lentils by about 2 inches. Place a lid on the saucepan and cook until the lentils are soft, not *al dente*. It is difficult to say how long that will take since it depends on the quality and freshness of the legumes, but lentils are usually ready within 1 hour. Check the liquid every now and then and add more broth whenever the lentils are too dry.
6 Add the rest of the broth and bring back to a boil. Mix in the rice and, if necessary, add more boiling broth. If you have used all the broth, pour in boiling water. The amount of liquid needed varies with the quality of the lentils, the kind of rice used, and the heat on which the soup is cooked. The resulting soup should be quite thick: lots of rice and lentils in a little liquid.

Serves 4–5

$\frac{1}{4}$ cup olive oil
1 small onion, very finely chopped
2 ounces smoked pancetta, cut into tiny pieces
1 small carrot
1 large celery stalk
1 sprig of fresh rosemary, about 2-inches long
1 garlic clove
salt and freshly ground black pepper
1 generous teaspoon tomato paste
$1\frac{1}{2}$ quarts vegetable broth or 2 vegetable bouillon cubes dissolved in the same amount of water
1 cup green lentils, rinsed and drained
nearly 1 cup Italian rice, preferably Vialone Nano
extra virgin olive oil for the table, a Tuscan or Roman oil

7 Season with lots of pepper, and simmer until the rice is *al dente* (15–20 minutes). Taste and adjust the seasoning. Serve the soup immediately, passing a bottle of extra virgin olive oil for everyone to pour a little over his serving of soup. Although not essential, I recommend this last *battesimo* – christening – because the oil livens up the earthy soup with its fruity flavor.

RISO CON LE VERDURE
RICE WITH VEGETABLES

Serves 6 as a first course or 4 as a main course

1 large boiling potato, diced
2 carrots, diced
1 large leek, white and green part, cut into rounds
$\frac{3}{4}$ cup shelled fresh peas or green beans, according to season
1 celery stalk, diced
1 zucchini, diced
salt and freshly ground black pepper
$1\frac{1}{4}$ cups Italian rice, preferably Vialone Nano
$\frac{1}{2}$ cup extra virgin olive oil
3 garlic cloves, minced
12 fresh sage leaves, chopped
2 large ripe tomatoes, peeled, seeded, and coarsely chopped
4oz Italian fontina or raclette cheese, diced
6 tablespoons freshly grated Parmesan cheese

Northern and southern Italy meet happily in this dish, which was given to me by the Neapolitan owner of a superb green-grocer in Valtellina, an Alpine valley north of Milan. The dish is halfway between a minestrone and a risotto with vegetables and yet it tastes different from either. The flavor of the vegetables comes through strongly, enhanced by the final *soffritto*.

1 Choose a large pot – I use my earthenware stockpot of 5 quarts capacity. Put all the washed and cut vegetables in it and add enough water to come three-quarters of the way up the side of the pot. Season with salt, bring to a boil, and simmer, uncovered, for 45 minutes.
2 Add the rice to the vegetables, stir well, and cook for about 15 minutes or until done. The vegetables should be nice and soft and the rice should be *al dente*, thus giving a pleasing contrast of texture.
3 While the rice is cooking, make a little *soffritto* (frying mixture). Heat the oil, garlic and sage in a small frying pan until the sage begins to sizzle and the aroma of the garlic to rise. Add the tomatoes and cook for 5 minutes, stirring occasionally.

4 When the rice is ready, drain the contents of the stockpot very well (you can keep the liquid for a soup) and transfer the rice and vegetable mixture, a ladleful at a time, to serving bowl. Dress each ladleful with a couple of spoonfuls of the *soffritto*, a handful of cheese cubes, a generous grinding of pepper, and a spoonful of Parmesan. Mix very thoroughly after each addition, and serve at once.

Note: By dressing the dish gradually, you make sure the *soffritto* and the cheese are equally distributed, as they should be.

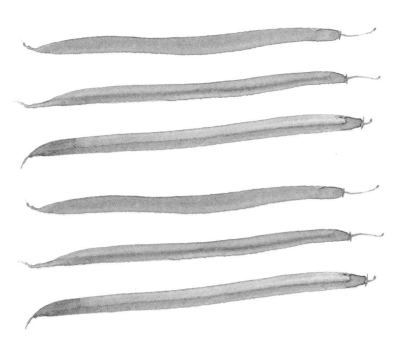

MINESTRA DI RISO, MANDORLE E PREZZEMOLO

──── RICE, ALMOND, AND PARSLEY SOUP ────

Serves 4

$\frac{3}{4}$ cup almonds
5 cups chicken broth
1 chicken breast half
$\frac{1}{2}$ cup Italian rice, preferably Vialone Nano
3 tablespoons chopped fresh flat-leaf Italian parsley
salt and freshly ground black pepper

No clear soup like this can be successful without the basis of a good homemade broth. For this recipe I suggest a chicken broth instead of the more usual meat broth.

This is a delicate soup to be served to people who appreciate the balance of good ingredients.

1 Heat the oven to 425°F.

2 Blanch the almonds in boiling water 30 seconds. Drain and peel them. Place the almonds on a baking sheet and bake until the aroma rises and the almonds are quite brown, about 10 minutes. Chop them to the size of grains of rice.

3 Heat the broth until boiling. Put in the chicken breast and cook over low heat 10 minutes. Lift the breast out of the broth and place on a board.

4 Slide the rice into the simmering broth. Simmer 10 minutes.

5 Skin and bone chicken breast. Cut the meat into small strips.

6 Stir the strips of chicken, the parsley, and almonds into the soup. Cook until the rice is *al dente*. Taste and add salt and pepper if necessary, then serve.

MINESTRONE

VEGETABLE SOUP WITH RICE

This is the classic minestrone with rice, or Minestrone alla Milanese, where rice is the starchy nourishment added to a vegetable soup.

1 Heat the oil and butter in a stockpot or a large saucepan, add the pancetta, and sauté 2 minutes. Add the onions, sage, and parsley and fry 5 minutes or so over low heat.

2 Mix in the garlic, carrots, celery, and potatoes and fry 2 minutes. Add the green beans and zucchini and sauté 2–3 minutes longer.

3 Cover with $2\frac{1}{2}$ quarts of hot water and add the tomatoes and salt and pepper to taste. Cover the pan and cook at a very low simmer a minimum of $1\frac{1}{2}$ hours. Minestrone can be cooked as long as 3 hours and it will be even better. Do not think that the vegetables will break up; they do not.

4 About 30 minutes before you want to eat, add the cabbage and cook 15 minutes. Then add the rice and canned beans and stir well. Continue cooking uncovered, at a steady simmer, until the rice is *al dente*. Serve with a bowl of Parmesan on the side.

Minestrone is even better made a day in advance and warmed up. In the summer it is delicious cold, though not straight from the refrigerator.

Serves 6

2 tablespoons olive oil
2 tablespoons butter
$\frac{1}{4}$ pound unsmoked pancetta, or unsmoked bacon, chopped
2 onions, coarsely chopped
4 or 5 fresh sage leaves, snipped
1 tablespoon chopped fresh flat-leaf Italian parsley
2 garlic cloves, chopped
2 carrots, diced
2 celery stalks, diced
2 potatoes, about $\frac{1}{2}$ pound, diced
$\frac{1}{4}$ pound green beans, cut into $\frac{3}{4}$ inch pieces
$\frac{1}{2}$ pound zucchini, diced
1 cup canned Italian plum tomatoes with their juice
salt and freshly ground black pepper
$\frac{1}{2}$ pound cabbage, cut into strips
$\frac{2}{3}$ cup Italian rice, preferably Berrifino Padano or Vialone Nano
14 ounces canned borlotti beans, drained
freshly grated Parmesan cheese, for serving

RIPIENI E INSALATE DI RISO

—— RICE STUFFINGS AND SALADS ——

Two recipes for rice stuffings hardly do justice to an array of dishes in which rice is the primary ingredient of the stuffing. But I have chosen my favorites. While rice is commonly used as a stuffing for vegetables, its use in stuffing fish is less usual. The recipe for squid stuffed with rice is very interesting and very good; in fact, it is my preferred way of stuffing squid.

The versatility of rice is boundless. It even makes excellent salads, which is more than can be said for pasta. I have also included in this section two of my favorite recipes for rice salads.

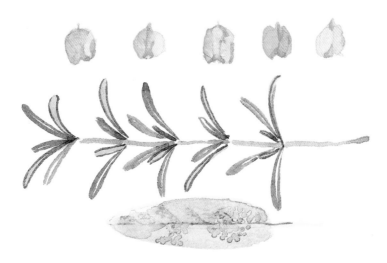

POMODORI RIPIENI DI RISO

TOMATOES STUFFED WITH BASIL-FLAVORED RICE

Serves 4 as a first course

1 pound ripe tomatoes, all the
same size
salt and freshly ground
black pepper
6 tablespoons Italian rice,
preferably Vialone Nano
2 garlic cloves, finely sliced
12 fresh basil leaves, snipped
1 egg
7 tablespoons extra virgin
olive oil

The rice in this recipe is not previously cooked, but only soaked in oil so that it retains a stronger flavor. By the end of the cooking the tomatoes are very soft and are amalgamated with the rice, rather than being separate ingredients.

1 Wash and dry the tomatoes. Cut them across in half. Scoop out some of the seeds and discard. Scoop out all the pulp and the juice with a pointed spoon, taking care not to break the skin. Chop the pulp and put it in a bowl with the juice.

2 Sprinkle the insides of the tomato halves with salt and chill them.

3 Add the rice to the bowl together with the garlic and basil.

4 Beat the egg very lightly and mix thoroughly into the rice mixture. Add the oil, plenty of pepper, and salt to taste. Mix again very well and let soak at least 3 hours.

5 Heat the oven to 375°F.

6 Oil a large baking dish and place the tomato halves in it, cut-side up. Fill them with the rice mixture, to come level with the tops of the tomatoes. Cover the dish with foil and bake until the rice is cooked, about 45 minutes. Serve hot.

CALAMARI RIPIENI DI RISO

SQUID STUFFED WITH RICE

Rice, a staple of the north, is sometimes used in fish dishes in Puglia, the heel of the Italian boot. The fish used there for this dish is cuttlefish. Although this is a fairly common species in many Mediterranean countries, as well as in Japan and India, it is rarely sold fresh here. For this reason I prefer to use squid, which are more readily available. Whenever I can I buy the local squid, large specimens with a very good flavour, much better than the small calamari which come from Italy and Spain. These are often frozen or, what is worse, appear to be fresh although in fact they have previously been frozen.

---

1 Ask your fish merchant to clean the squid, or do it yourself by following these instructions. Hold the sac in one hand and pull off the tentacles with the other hand. The contents of the sac will come out, too. Cut the tentacles above the eyes. Squeeze out the thin bony beak in the center of the tentacles. Peel off the skin from the sac and the flap. Remove the translucent backbone from inside the sac and rinse the sac and tentacles under cold water. Keep the sacs whole.

2 Cut the tentacles into small pieces and then chop them coarsely until they are about the same size as the grains of rice.

3 Put 2 tablespoons of the oil in a sauté pan. Add the rice, chopped tentacles, parsley, garlic, chili pepper, and lemon zest and sauté briskly a few minutes to *insaporire* – let the mixture take up all the flavors.

4 Finely chop the anchovy fillets and stir into the mixture. Cook at a lower temperature 1 minute or so. Taste and add salt and pepper, if necessary.

5 Heat the oven to 350°F.

Serves 3–4 as a main course

4 large squid, about $2\frac{1}{4}$ pounds
6 tablespoons olive oil
$\frac{1}{4}$ cup cooked Italian rice,
preferably Vialone Nano
3 tablespoons chopped fresh
flat-leaf Italian parsley
2 garlic cloves, chopped
$\frac{1}{2}$ small dried chili pepper,
chopped
grated zest of $\frac{1}{2}$ unwaxed lemon
2 salted anchovies, boned and
rinsed, or 4 canned anchovy
fillets, drained
salt and freshly ground
black pepper
$\frac{1}{2}$ cup dry white wine

6 Fill each squid sac with the rice mixture. Do not pack the stuffing too tight or the sac will burst during the cooking. Stitch up the opening with a needle and thread and lay the squid in a single layer, close to each other, in a baking dish. (I use a metal pan, because metal transmits the heat better than ceramic.)

7 Pour the rest of the oil and the wine over the squid. Cover the dish tightly with a piece of foil and bake until the squid are tender when pricked with a fork, about 1 hour.

8 When they are done, transfer the squid to a carving board and let cool 10 minutes. Slice off a very thin strip from the sewn end to eliminate the thread. Cut each sac into slices about 1-inch thick. If you possess one, use an electric carving knife which will make this slicing very easy. Otherwise see that your knife is very sharp. Gently transfer the slices to a serving dish.

9 Taste the cooking juices. If bland, boil briskly until reduced and full of flavor. Spoon over the squid. You can serve the dish hot, warm, or even at room temperature, which I personally prefer.

INSALATA DI RISO CON MOZZARELLA ED ACCIUGHE

RICE SALAD WITH MOZZARELLA AND ANCHOVY
FILLETS

I strongly recommend using buffalo mozzarella for this dish. If possible, dress the rice 2 hours before serving.

1 Cook the rice in plenty of boiling salted water until just *al dente*. (Remember that when served cold, rice is better if a touch undercooked.) Drain the rice, rinse under cold water, and drain again. Transfer the rice to a bowl and pat dry with paper towels. Add 2 tablespoons of the oil and let cool.

2 Chop the eggs and add to the rice, together with the mozzarella.

3 Chop the anchovy fillets and place in another bowl. Mix in the parsley, garlic, and chili pepper. Beat in the remaining oil with a fork until the sauce thickens. Season with salt and pepper to taste.

4 Spoon this dressing into the rice and mix very thoroughly with two forks so as to separate all the grains. Taste and adjust the seasoning to your liking. Scatter the olives and capers here and there and serve cold, but not chilled.

Serves 4 as a first course

1 cup Italian rice, preferably
Vialone Nano
salt and freshly ground
black pepper
6 tablespoons extra virgin
olive oil
2 hard-boiled eggs
5 ounces buffalo mozzarella, cut
into small cubes
6 salted anchovies, boned and
rinsed, or 12 canned anchovy
fillets, drained
$\frac{1}{4}$ cup chopped fresh flat-leaf
Italian parsley
1 small garlic clove, minced
1 small dried chili pepper,
seeded and crumbled
12 black olives
1 tablespoon capers, rinsed and
dried

RISO E CECI IN INSALATA

RICE AND CHICK PEA SALAD

Serves 4

⅔ cup dried chick peas (garbanzo beans)
salt and freshly ground black pepper
1 teaspoon baking soda
1 tablespoon flour
1 small onion
1 celery stalk
2 sprigs of rosemary
4 fresh sage leaves
a few parsley stems
2 garlic cloves
7 tablespoons extra virgin olive oil
nearly 1 cup Italian rice, preferably Vialone Nano or Semifino Padano
1 garlic clove, minced
a lovely bunch of fresh flat-leaf Italian parsley, finely chopped
½ pound ripe tomatoes, peeled and seeded
12 fresh basil leaves, snipped

I t is surprising how two ingredients as modest as rice and chick peas can produce, when mixed together, such a really good and attractive dish.

Cook the chick peas until they are soft. In common with my compatriots, I find nothing more unpleasant than undercooked legumes, as they are sometimes served in Italian restaurants outside Italy. The rice should be *al dente*, not because of the over-praised "contrast of texture," but simply because rice is good *al dente*. Chick peas, however, are best when soft.

1 Put the chick peas in a large bowl and cover with plenty of cold water. Mix the salt, baking soda, and flour with a little cold water to make a paste and stir this into the soaking water. This helps to tenderize the skin as well as the chick peas themselves. Let soak at least 18 hours; 24 is better.

2 Rinse the chick peas and put them in a pot. (An earthenware stockpot is the best for cooking legumes because of earthenware's heat-retaining properties.) Add the onion and celery and cover with water to come about 3 inches over the chick peas. Place the pot on the heat.

3 Tie the rosemary, sage, parsley stems, and whole garlic cloves in a small piece of cheesecloth to make a bundle and add to the pot. Bring to a boil, then lower the heat and cook, covered, until the chick peas are ready. The liquid should simmer rather than boil. Chick peas take 2–3 hours to cook. Add salt only when they are nearly done, as the salt tends to make the skin crack and wrinkle.

4 Drain the chick peas (you can keep the liquid for a bean or vegetable soup). Remove and discard the onion, celery, and herb bag. Transfer the chick peas to a bowl and toss, while still hot, with 2 tablespoons of the oil.

5 Cook the rice in plenty of boiling salted water. Drain when just *al dente*. Mix into the chick peas.

6 Put the rest of the oil, the chopped garlic, and chopped parsley in a small frying pan. Sauté 2 minutes, stirring constantly.

7 Dice the tomatoes and mix into the *soffritto* – frying mixture. Cook 1 minute and then spoon over the rice and chick pea mixture. Add the snipped fresh basil and plenty of pepper. Toss thoroughly but lightly. Taste and check the salt. Serve at room temperature.

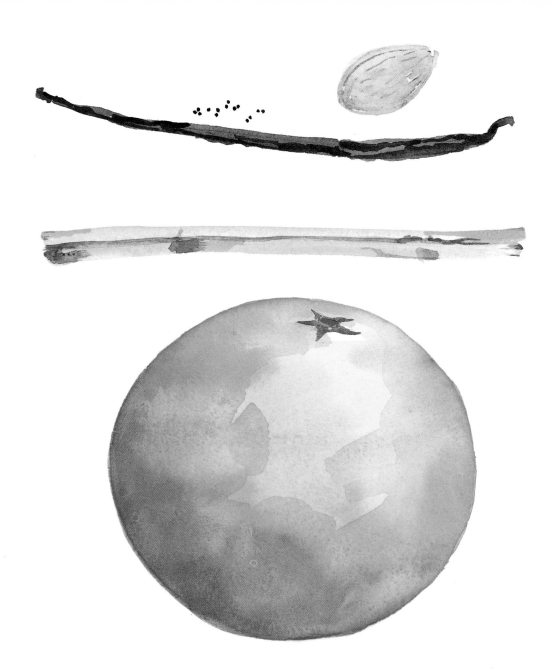

RISI DOLCI

This little book of homage to my home town's staple food ends with three recipes for desserts, although, ironically, they do not come from Milan. The rice cake and rice fritters are from Tuscany and the Black Rice is from Sicily.

TORTA DI RISO

RICE CAKE WITH ALMONDS AND
RAISINS

Serves 8

3 cups whole milk
nearly 1 cup sugar
a strip of unwaxed lemon zest,
yellow part only
a piece of vanilla bean, 1-inch
long
a piece of cinnamon stick,
2-inches long
a pinch of salt
$\frac{2}{3}$ cup Italian rice, preferably
Arborio
$\frac{1}{4}$ cup golden raisins
2 tablespoons dark rum
$\frac{2}{3}$ cup almonds, blanched and
peeled (see page 40)
4 eggs, separated
grated zest of $\frac{1}{2}$ unwaxed lemon
enough butter and dry bread
crumbs for coating the bottom
of the pan
a sprinkle of confectioners'
sugar, to finish

This is the Florentine version of a cake that is popular all over central Italy. I like to make it with Arborio rice, as it swells during the cooking while absorbing the milk. You can add other ingredients according to your taste, for instance chocolate pieces and/or candied peel. What you will have is a firm yet moist cake, not a pudding, that is equally delicious with a dollop or two of thick cream on top or without cream. The cake should not be served until at least the day after making it, to let the flavors blend.

1 Put the milk, $2\frac{1}{2}$ tablespoons of the sugar, the strip of lemon zest, vanilla bean, cinnamon stick, and a pinch of salt in a saucepan and bring to a boil. Add the rice and stir well with a wooden spoon. Cook, uncovered, over very low heat, stirring frequently, until the rice has absorbed the milk and is soft, about 35 minutes. Set aside to cool.

2 Heat the oven to 350°F.

3 Put the golden raisins in a bowl and pour over the rum. Let them puff up.

4 Spread the almonds on a baking sheet and toast them in the oven until they are quite brown, about 10 minutes. Shake the sheet occasionally to prevent them from burning. Cool them a little, then chop them coarsely.

5 Remove the strip of lemon zest, the vanilla bean, and cinnamon stick from the rice and spoon the rice into a mixing bowl. (Wash and dry the vanilla bean so that you can use it again.) Incorporate 1 egg yolk at a time into the rice, mixing well after each addition. Add the remaining sugar, the almonds, golden raisins with the

rum, and the grated lemon zest to the rice and egg mixture and mix everything together thoroughly.

6 Beat the egg whites until they are stiff, then fold them gently into the rice mixture.

7 Butter an 8-inch springform cake pan. Line the bottom with wax paper and butter the paper. Sprinkle all over with bread crumbs to coat evenly and shake out excess crumbs.

8 Spoon the rice mixture into the prepared pan. Bake in the oven (still at the same temperature) until a thin skewer or a wooden toothpick inserted in the middle of the cake comes out just moist, about 45 minutes. The cake should also have shrunk from the side of the pan.

9 Let the cake cool in the pan, then remove the clipped side and turn the cake over onto a plate. Remove the base of the pan and the lining paper. Place a round serving platter on the cake and turn it over again. Leave for at least 24 hours before serving the cake. Sprinkle with confectioners' sugar before serving.

RISO NERO

—————— BLACK RICE PUDDING ——————

Serves 6

2½ cups whole milk
⅓ cup Italian rice, preferably
Vialone Nano
7 tablespoons sugar
⅔ cup almonds, blanched,
peeled, and chopped
pinch of salt
pinch of ground cinnamon
⅔ cup black coffee
1½ ounces semisweet chocolate,
flaked or grated
grated zest of 1 small orange
1 tablespoon unsalted butter
⅔ cup whipping cream

There are not many rice dishes in Sicily, but this is one of the few Sicilian contributions to the vast range of Italian rice desserts. It is different from the rice desserts of the central Italian regions – the motherland of rice cakes and puddings – because it contains a high proportion of chocolate and coffee.

In Sicily, this dish is served without cream, but even though I am not a cream fan, I must admit that cream lightens the almondy-chocolate flavor of the riso nero.

———————————————

1 Put the milk, rice, sugar, almonds, salt, cinnamon, and coffee in a heavy-bottomed saucepan. Bring to a boil and simmer until the rice is very soft, about 1 hour, stirring frequently. If you use a heat diffuser you can leave it a little longer, but be careful because the milky rice tends to stick to the bottom of the pan.
2 Remove the pan from the heat and mix in the chocolate and orange zest.
3 Grease a 1-quart pudding basin or other dome-shaped mold with the butter. Spoon in the rice mixture and let cool. When cold, cover with plastic wrap and put in the refrigerator to chill.
4 Free the pudding all around with a long metal spatula and unmold it onto a round platter.
5 Whip the cream and spread it all over the brown dome just before serving.

ANTICA E RINOMATA RISERIA

FERRON

(La famosa "Pila Vecchia")
FONDATA NEL 1650

ISOLA DELLA SCALA
VERONA
IL RISO CHE FA BUONI SANGUE

RISO SEMIFINO
VIALONE NANO
RICE FOR RISOTTO

Product of Italy
PESO NETTO 1000 g ℮
NET WEIGHT: 85 2 oz (2.2 lbs)

FRITTELLE DI RISO

RICE FRITTERS

Serves 4

2½ cups whole milk
pinch of salt
⅓ cup Italian rice,
preferably Semifino Padano or
Vialone Nano
2 tablespoons sugar
pared zest of ½ unwaxed orange,
in strips
pared zest of ½ unwaxed lemon,
in strips
2 extra large eggs
a little vegetable oil for frying
a sprinkle of confectioners'
sugar for decoration

These fritters are sold and eaten in the streets of Florence as a *merenda*, or snack.

1 Put the milk, salt, rice, sugar, and fruit zest in a heavy-bottomed saucepan. Bring slowly to a boil, stirring frequently. Cook, uncovered, on a very low heat until the rice has absorbed all the milk and is very soft, about 1 hour. Stir frequently. Spoon the mixture into a bowl and let it cool a little.

2 Lightly beat the eggs to break the white, then incorporate into the rice mixture. Mix very well and place the bowl in the refrigerator. If possible, chill 1 hour so the mixture firms, which will make it easier to shape and fry.

3 Heat the oil to 325°F in a wok or a deep frying pan. At this temperature, a piece of stale bread should brown in 50 seconds.

4 With a metal spoon pick up some of the rice mixture – a dollop about the size of a large walnut – and with the help of a second spoon slide it into the oil. Fry the fritters in batches until they are golden on both sides. Retrieve them with a slotted metal spatula and place on paper towels to drain.

5 Sprinkle each fritter very generously with confectioners' sugar before serving. They are good hot or cold.